RESURRECTION!
Trusting the God I Knew with a Future I Didn't

Rick Manis

Empyrion Publishing
PO Box 784327
Winter Garden FL 34778

RESURRECTION! Trusting the God I Knew, with a Future I Didn't

Copyright © 2014 by Rick Manis

ISBN: 978-0692328187

Empyrion Publishing
PO Box 784327
Winter Garden FL 34778
info@EmpyrionPublishing.com

Unless otherwise noted, all Scripture quotations are from the New King James Version of the Bible.

The New International Version is noted as: NIV

The Message is noted as MSG

Bold type is added by the author for emphasis.

Printed in the United States of America

Introduction

It's been a few years since I've written a book. Since my last book, *"Glory in the Glass,"* I have gone through the most trying time of my life. I experienced something I never dreamed I would. My lovely wife of 33 years left this world.

My ministry over the years has been a voice of victory and the kind of faith that overcomes this world. As I dealt with my life situation, there would have to be answers to the obvious questions that surround such a tragic blow.

This book does give answers for the one who has suffered a setback. It doesn't answer all of the theological questions, but it definitely gives the correct answers to the loss you may have felt.

I have been very patient in writing this book. Though I immediately wanted to pen my experience, and people immediately requested that I write a book on the revelations I received during this season, it seemed that the Lord wanted me to wait for the dust to settle while I continued to rise from my ashes.

In these pages are words of resurrection power. This is the most positive book I've written, and also the most personal. I've written with the joy that has come from my Father as He has proved Himself faithful and true to His Word. I have experienced the true power of resurrection!

However, this encouragement comes with much empathy. I know first-hand the shock of losing, and the joy that comes from getting the last laugh. I know both my abject weakness and my unlimited power that comes from God.

If you've suffered loss, and are finding it hard to get going again, this is for you. Your high praises are about to sound. You are about to enter more joy and goodness than you have ever imagined you could. You are about to experience your RESURRECTION.

Forward!

CONTENTS

1. Nightmare on Fullness Street 7

2. My Wonderful Counselor 15

3. Time to Get Up 21

4. If I Can Do It, You Can Do It 27

5. The Power of Resurrection 33

6. Resurrection in Earth Life 41

7. Don't Dismiss the Now
   by Missing Your Past 47

8. The God I Knew
   and the Future I Didn't 53

9. Resurrection Covers Your Losses 59

CHAPTER 1

Nightmare on Fullness Street

The doctor's words shot into our ears and careened wildly and repeatedly like a pinball in our heads: *cancer, advanced, metastatic, stage four...*

The scan was showing multiple tumors throughout her abdomen. The words delivered what amounted to a medical death sentence for my precious wife, Teresa.

How could this be? She had no symptoms other than the dull ache in her side that seemed like a pulled muscle. The doctor told her that it was probably just a muscle pull, but he wanted a scan just to be sure. The scan revealed the creeping, growing assassin hiding secretly inside. This visit to the doctor's office had launched a nightmare that seemed too horrible to be true.

Teresa was a stunning woman with dark hair and beautiful dark eyes. Her smile was like sunshine. Her heart was sweet and pure. Her outer beauty was only surpassed by her inner beauty. She was totally in love with God, and was known for her mercy and kindness toward people.

We honestly felt many times like we were the ultimate couple. Even in our middle age we were lovebirds, totally happy to be with each other every minute of our lives. We were not ashamed of expressing our love for each other, and we did so countless times each day. We were blessed in so many ways. We had beautiful children and grandchildren. We worked together in my ministry, and we were very fulfilled by the work. We lived in a beautiful home, Teresa's dream house that we had built just three years earlier. We were youthful and seemingly healthy.

But this day with the doctor would mark the beginning of a three year battle that we would not win. It would be a battle that would take my wife, along with my dreams, my money, sometimes my sanity, and even the hope of my future.

The Three Year Ordeal

Teresa was adamant that I not share our battle with anyone. She didn't want anyone worrying about her or feeling sorry for her. She didn't want to deal with the looks and questions from people. Also, she felt that the most effective way to fight the fight of faith would be to keep it between her and myself, and God.

Her first surgery was an eight hour marathon that removed multiple tumors from her diaphragm down to her pelvic bone. A total hysterectomy was done, as well as the removal of other organs and parts of organs. In respect of Teresa's wishes, I disclosed to others only that she had a hysterectomy. This was the first of many times I would only share a partial truth of her condition.

Over the next three years I would become experienced in many nursing skills. After her surgery I packed her infected incision twice daily. I administered shots. Her pain management became an art and a three-way tug-of-war between Teresa, me, and the doctors/nurses. Meds, restroom, cleanliness and countless other needs made sleepless nights the norm. Constant calls with questions for the doctor and emergency room trips marked what once, was a life on cruise control.

I canceled many ministry trips while Teresa recovered from surgery. Afterward, chemotherapy kept her dependent on me much of the time.

I loved Teresa and didn't feel that I was sacrificing or being asked to do something unreasonable. I only wanted her well, and I was committed to doing anything and everything in my ability to see it through. Any hardship I experienced was nothing compared to what my lovely wife was going through both physically and mentally. (She was such a warrior!) But I do want to paint an accurate picture of my own experience because I know that many people go through things that seem to be more than they can handle. Believe me. I can totally relate.

After a time of remission, the cancer showed up on Teresa's spine and it came with a vengeance. There would be more surgery, more chemo, radiation, and more complications. She would lose her ability to walk, and later, to breathe on her own. I managed oxygen calibration and dangerously high doses of pain medications. I fed her and carried her to the toilet. Sleep would come in very short intervals at best.

It really was overwhelming so much of the time. I sometimes felt my mind would snap. I wanted to fall on the floor and cry. My soul cried out for rest, but I was Teresa's source of inspiration. I constantly spoke positive, hopeful words to her. I tried to answer all of her questions and fears with encouragement. I also had to keep encouraging myself in the Lord.

I sincerely thought we would get through all of this and Teresa would be well. I thought so until nearly the very end, but ultimately she stepped into Heaven.

"What the hell, Lord!"

I will pause at this point and address some questions people may have about the death of my wife. I preach about fullness, and I believe in such a high standard of overcoming faith and life that the questions are certainly understandable. I testify that I've not had the flu or a headache since 1982 and don't believe I ever will again. So how could this happen?

First, we all have our own individual walk with God that has nothing to do with another person, no matter how close we are. Teresa had a close walk with the Lord. She had her own personal revelations and enviable experiences with Him. It's possible that at some point in the battle, the opportunity to leave a body overwhelmed with pain is presented. The details of her final hours leave me to believe that this was what happened.

Second, I have always allowed room to grow in my belief. Knowing God's ultimate will allows us to grow in the knowledge of it, and we are all growing in this knowledge. It doesn't mean that our vision is wrong, but we continue to behold His glory and be changed. My belief in fullness has affected my life in ways not possible unless I had embraced that truth. I am however, continuing to know and grow in fullness.

So do we throw it all away because of a loss, or do we go forward and grow more into it? We go forward. Though I would have a serious talk with the Lord about my ministry, I was never much confused about it because I have always been aware that we are growing, and in the future we will see even more and greater victories because of the truth of the finished work of Christ.

On a few occasions I've been asked if I was ever angry, or did I ever say, "What the hell, Lord!"

The honest answer is no. By this time in my life, I had come to know the grace of God in a beautiful way. My relationship with Him is not volatile. I knew I could trust Him going forward, and I simply went to Him for comfort and guidance. Sure, there were things I didn't quite understand, but getting in the flesh over it would not be productive, so I would walk in the Spirit, and I would have peace in God. I would let Him have my back. I would let Him take me to my future. I would enjoy God's mercy and goodness while I was in the valley of the shadow of death.

Teresa was gone. Next for me would be the strangeness of such a catastrophic loss. I thank the Lord that He had prepared me over the years to walk in victory in this very situation.

I would grieve, but it would be as a son of God, and not as a son of Adam.

Resurrection!

CHAPTER 2

My Wonderful Counselor

"...do not grieve like the rest of mankind, who have no hope." – I Thessalonians 4:13 NIV

I cried vehemently the morning Teresa passed away. By afternoon, my crying had given way to numbness. Friends and relatives flocked around me, keeping me company and taking care of errands for me. The unreal reality was a strange feeling. It helped to have people around, but alone at night the tears would return. For the next few days I was in shock. I was quite functional, but it seemed I was moving in slow motion.

I had been the company and counsel many times for numerous people in this situation. Now I was the one making decisions on funeral arrangements that had to be made quickly while in shock.

Now I had to remember my own counsel to those I had helped before. My basic exhortation to others was that it's right to sorrow and not pretend everything is alright, but by the same token, not to continue in a spirit of grief that is unhealthy. I was determined to let the grieving process do its work so I would have no lingering damage from this experience. I would simply allow the Lord to counsel me and walk me through.

The first thing my Wonderful Counselor taught me was to be grateful. He spoke this to me the day after Teresa left. God told me that sorrow lingers in people who dwell on what they've lost rather than what they have. So I was to dwell on what I had gained from Teresa instead of what I had lost.

I realized that I had been blessed by the Lord for nearly thirty-four years with the love of a wonderful woman. I was blessed with an amazing marriage experience. It was a blessing that many live without, but I had it. The Lord didn't have to give it to me, but He did. Gratitude began to dominate my thoughts, and self pity had no place in me. When words of sympathy were graciously extended to me by my friends I could thank them, then I could smile and speak of how blessed I really was. They would sometimes mention how they marveled at my strength, but I owe it all to my Counselor. I could already feel myself rising, though I still felt kind of disoriented.

Friends were wonderful to me, and I do feel as though I have the best. Those who knew me well knew that I needed company. They knew that I needed to laugh, and they knew I needed to get out and enjoy life. They were so good about spending time with me and taking me places. It helped tremendously to feel like I was still in the game. It reminded me that life goes on, and it would go on with me.

My Wonderful Counselor was telling me that I had to give myself the right to laugh, the right to have fun, and the right to enjoy life; so I allowed myself to do just that when I was with my friends. It was when I was alone at night in my big empty house that the strangeness of being alone would be my reality and I would miss my precious wife.

The strangest thing was the change in everything. It seemed that my world was gone. I couldn't see my future.

I didn't know how long the grieving process would be, and with all of the other questions I had about my life and ministry I began to cancel some of my ministry engagements. I thought it might be wise to take a little sabbatical, but I just didn't know. I did know that I wasn't in any condition to be in the pulpit at the present time. In my numbness, I couldn't imagine what I would say.

Everything was a little strange, but I was very aware that the Lord was with me all of the time. Though it looked like I was in a place of nothingness, I knew that He was awesome and that He would get me through this in a powerful way. Though I couldn't imagine what my life would now be like, I had hope and I would go forward with the Lord. I was convinced of these things because of my years of walking with God and seeing Him get me through every trial I ever had. It was just hard to get a picture of my future. I didn't know what my life or ministry would look like.

A couple of days after Teresa's passing I spoke with a pastor where I was scheduled to speak in just a few days. His church was only an hour from my home, and when I asked him if we were still on for that night he said it was up to me. I told him I would let him know in a day or two.

Teresa's graduation service was amazing. It did what every funeral should do. It was a joyful celebration of her life, of salvation, hope, and ultimate victory over death. It was powerful and everyone felt good by the end of it. It gave me and the family a sense of closure. Now it was time to move forward, and the next day the Lord would show me something that would bring such joy and strength to me. It would stand me upon my feet. It would put a fire in my heart. It would set my face toward a glorious future.

I called the pastor and told him I would be there to preach at his church. I had a message!

Resurrection!

CHAPTER 3

Time to Get Up

"Moses my servant is dead. Get going. Cross this Jordan River..." Joshua 1:2 MSG

The day after Teresa's service, my Wonderful Counselor spoke to me and told me to get up and move forward. He said that He had a purpose for the rest of my life and I should now get on with it.

Knowing the will of God in a situation like this is a very important thing. Otherwise we will grieve like the world grieves. We will grieve like those who have no hope (I Thessalonians 4:13). It helps to know that the Lord doesn't want us to keep hurting, and He wants us to wash our face and get on with life. This should be normal for a Christian. It's how we should roll in the kingdom of God.

When Moses died it looked like the journey was over for all the Israelites. Moses was the best leader ever. It was usually difficult enough to move forward even *with* Moses. Now what would happen? Abort the mission? Go back to Egypt? Curl up and die in the wilderness? Cry about it for a few years?

God only allowed them one month to mourn, and *those* were people who were not new creations in Christ. They didn't have the kingdom of righteousness, peace, and joy in the Holy Ghost abiding in them. After this short time, the Lord commanded Joshua to get up and go forward. God had plans and mourning wasn't part of them. Israel was going to the Promised Land and they would do better than they ever did with Moses.

In another instance, the Lord told Samuel to quit mourning for Saul (I Samuel 16:1). God had something better on the horizon and Samuel needed to get on with it. *Something better* turned out to be David, though nobody could have predicted that.

When you lose someone or something important to you, it's hard to see how life could ever be as good as it was, especially when it seems you've lost the best there could ever be. That was the case for me when I lost Teresa. I had the best. I felt that I might go on with life, but it would never be as good as it was before. This sense of loss and hopelessness can dominate you until it becomes almost a part of your identity. Your days will contain an endless cycle of *"woe is me"* unless you know the truth that makes you free.

God is Not in the Earthquake

It is *truth* that makes us free and nothing else. Often, in sorrow, people wonder when God is going to make the sorrow stop. They wonder when He will finally heal their broken heart. They feel confused about their situation and about the Lord. They believe He can deliver them from their hurt, but they wonder why He hasn't yet. Then they can settle into a surmising that it must be God's will to keep them in sorrow for some unknown reason, or they just think it is normal to be in that condition. They sit in their soul jail waiting for God to show up and break them out.

Elijah was doing that in I Kings 19. He was in such sorrow and self pity that he begged the Lord to take his life. Elijah just felt like he wanted to die. He didn't see a future anymore. He said *"It is enough"* (v. 4).

A strong wind came, breaking rocks on the mountain, but the Lord was not in the wind. After the wind, came an earthquake, but the Lord was not in the earthquake. A fire came, but the Lord was not in the fire.

Then there came a still small voice simply calling Elijah out of the cave. All the man needed was to hear the Word of the Lord. The Word is near us.

It's in our hearts. The Lord speaks to us from within, and that is where our deliverance is found. It's in the truth within us.

People usually are looking outward for their deliverance. They relate to God that way, and they want Him to make the circumstance good before they can come out of their cave. They feel incomplete and they want God to bring completeness to them. Truthfully, we *are* complete in Him. What a revelation! We have all that we need already, so we can move forward anytime we want to if we know the truth about ourselves.

As new creatures in Christ we are not victims of anything. We are supernaturally endowed with the Word and power of an overcoming life! When we are knocked down we get up and go with gusto. Creation is anxious to see the kind of people we really are. We are ambassadors of Heaven, and the things of this old world do not affect us the same way as those who have no hope. We are just different.

But sometimes I think most Christians relate more to unregenerate souls than they do to Jesus.

I remember speaking at a men's retreat for a particular church once. There was what I would describe as a "moping" spirit about the gathering. These men were all accustomed to being in touch with their feelings in such a way that everyone seemed to be aware of how pitiful they were. Each man's failures were highlighted, and each shortcoming was attended to with compassion, words of understanding, hugs, and lots of prayers. Apparently these retreats were a place where men could feel safe being vulnerable, which is good; but there was no real healing happening, only lots of tenderness.

I spoke about the fullness of God as usual. Afterward, men came forward in need of ministry. The first man spoke of the hurt he was still feeling from a split that happened in their church a few months previous. People had left the church and he couldn't get over it.

I began to tell him how to look at it so that peace, joy, and forgiveness comes easy.

While I was explaining things I was interrupted by the pastor who said to me, *"Rick, I appreciate all that you are saying, but I think this man is trying to tell us that he is grieving."*

The man then looked gratefully at his pastor and nodded his head, uttering *"Thank you."*

I knew the man was grieving. He virtually said as much. I felt his pain and wanted to give him a simple truth that would end the turmoil.

But these were people taught to love the grieving "process." I realized that I had nothing to offer them and turned it over to the pastor. Prayers were then offered requesting that God would allow the grieving process to run its course. Others stepped up for similar prayers. It went on and on.

God is always in the now, and we are complete in Him. It is the will of God that we arise from our hurts quickly.

Teresa had left, and was present with the Lord. She was now experiencing the fullness of unending love and joy. I had honored her and cared for her in her earth life. I had made it my mission to love her and to make her feel that she was treated better than any other woman. Now, things would never be the same, and I had to accept that. I had no regrets. I had to wash my face. I had to live.

It was time for my own resurrection!

CHAPTER 4

If I Can Do It
You Can Do It

I was told by someone that it really takes years to completely get over the grief and get back to "normal." Another said that even after a year waves of sorrow would hit me when I least expect it. They spoke from their own experience with the loss of a spouse.

My experience was very different from theirs. While my sorrow was very deep and intense, and there were internal issues that needed to be dealt with, it was a very swift resurrection for me. Some say God did a special, extraordinary miracle for me; but I see it as the natural result of a heart influenced by knowing God for many years. There was almost no way that I could stay in sorrow long. I had too much truth in me. The supernatural course of my life said I would not be at the mercy of even the most painful and hopeless of situations.

I've known and believed for quite a while that all things are possible with God. I've learned that there is nothing we cannot triumph in, so when my toughest moment in life came I was equipped with an overcoming attitude. My ear was inclined to hear that sweet and powerful voice of the Spirit, the voice of victory. Our agreement with that voice is the secret of our resurrection.

It's Not Our Strength

The truth makes us free, not our strength or will power. Nobody is strong enough to overcome this world. The power is in agreement with God.

I had no strength. My will was numbed. My future could not be imagined. However, I was not without hope and help.

We don't have to be strong, but we can choose life. This is the first thing to know when you are in a circumstance that seems too strong for you. We are not called to muscle our way through. We are called to choose life. We choose. God does the rest!

*"...I have set before you life and death, blessing and cursing; therefore **choose** life..."* - Deuteronomy 30:19

*"**Commit** your way to the Lord, trust also in Him, and He shall bring it to pass."* - Psalm 37:5

Without strength or knowledge of what lay in my future, I could choose blessing. My life would be blessed, and I would not be a sad loser. I would arise with hope and joy, and the Lord's blessing would make all of the difference!

It's Not in Our Natural Inborn Qualities

It's often explained that grieving time is different for everyone because everyone's personality is different. While that is very true on the surface, we need to realize that *truth* will actually change our personalities.

This is good news! It means we are not doomed to a longer sorrow than the next guy simply because of something we were born with.

Let's understand that life is not fair. We are not all born into equal situations. We are not born into equal intellect, talents, or physical abilities. We are not all born into nurturing families, or families with the financial resources to give us a head start.

BUT Jesus is the great equalizer! Because all things are possible in Him, none of us are really at a disadvantage. We simply need to know the will of God so we can agree with it. Agreement establishes a thing on the earth. In other words, it brings about heavenly manifestations!

So… if it's God's will that some are depressed for a few days and others stay depressed for a few years, then many of us are without hope and we are just going to zombie around for a while until our sentence is over.

BUT… If we know it's God's will that we *all* have everlasting joy, then we can agree with it. We can embrace it. We can *expect* it!

Some have suggested that I recovered quickly because I was born with a happy, positive personality.

LOL!! If people only knew what my personality was like before it was changed by the Word of God.

I grew up an angry, temperamental child. In my adult years, even as a Christian I was called a *melancholy* soul on more than a couple of occasions. Hurt and rejection had formed a large part of my personality.

But once I really knew that God absolutely loved me, once I knew that He had only good will for me and I was created to walk in the fullness of life, I GOT HAPPY! My outlook on life became positive. I became Mr. Optimistic. I gained a super power that always allowed me to see the good in everything and everyone. I was changed, and I became a people person. I was finally comfortable in my own skin. I became confident and loving and gracious.

When people meet me, they assume I was born with this personality, but it was formed by heavenly truth.

It's Really Not Even a Miracle

Our walk with God is supernatural and powerful, but I pull back from calling my resurrection a *miracle* because it lends the idea that it was specific to me and not necessarily available to any and all Christians.

Our power is God *in* us, not outside of us. When we need the power of God to change our situation, we aren't looking for a deliverance that comes to us from the outside. The kingdom of heaven comes from the inside out. Right thinking is what makes the difference!

God wanted me up and running, just like He wants everyone up and running; but if we think like common men we will be mentally crippled like common men.

CHAPTER 5

The Power of Resurrection

When I preached my first sermon a mere week after Teresa's passing, I spoke with power and authority. People commented on the depth of my ministry that night. They also commented on my personal inner strength that enabled me to show up the way I did.

But in reality I wasn't aware of any strength that I had. I told them I wasn't there that night because I had pulled myself up by my bootstraps. I wasn't there because of my will power. I looked strong simply because I knew something. It was something Abraham knew. It was something Jesus knew, and it was something Paul knew. It was something that overcomes the most intense of trials.

It was the power of resurrection!

Abraham's Test

Genesis 22:1 says that God tested Abraham, who was told by the Lord to offer his son, Isaac, as a burnt offering to God. But what really was the test?

Most would say it was a test of Abraham's faith, or his love and devotion toward God, but I see a different test, a much bigger test than any of these.

I submit to you that the test wasn't about how much faith or strength Abraham could muster to complete the task. It wasn't a test of how strong Abraham's will power would be. It wasn't even a test to see if Abraham loved God more than his own son.

God is really not interested in how much strength we have. He is our strength. He is really not interested in how much love we can feel toward Him. For years I wanted and tried to love God more. We can't do it by trying. He loves us first, and when we know that, we love Him automatically. It's never about our ability, strength, or proof of devotion. It's all about Him!

So the test is never to prove how good we are. It actually proves how good God is. And this test with Abraham would do just that.

The Lord told Abraham to go to the land of Moriah and offer Isaac on a mountain that God would show him. So Abraham went, not knowing everything he would need to know. Before he could complete the task, he would have to know something that only God could reveal. Abraham started off with raw obedience as he always did. He didn't know all he would need to know, but God promised to show it to him. Abraham would get a revelation from the Lord.

When we don't have the revelation necessary to see us through our situation, we have questions, maybe confusion. We may keep going forward, but we are not completely comfortable. We become anxious and sometimes frustrated.

I can imagine the questions in Abe's mind:
What is God doing?
Why is God requiring still more from me?
When will it ever be enough?
What about the promise He made, was I wrong about that?
Why doesn't He just explain it to me?

Finally, after three days of this, Abraham looked and he saw the place far off.

Notice that he didn't just stumble onto it and recognize it. He knew where it was while he was still far from it. Abraham got a revelation from God. The Lord showed him something that was going to change everything! Abraham saw something that immediately changed him. You can hear the positive tone in his voice, almost with excitement when he turns to tell his assistants what he is about to do!

*"And Abraham said to his young men, 'Stay here with the donkey; the lad and I will go yonder and worship, **and we will come back to you.**"* – Genesis 22:5

Whatever Abraham saw had made it all clear! He was not going to lose his boy. They were going to come back! Abraham had seen what he needed to see in order to complete the task. He saw the resurrection.

"By faith Abraham, when he was tested, offered up Isaac... concluding that God was able to raise him up, even from the dead..." - Hebrews 11:17-19

Abraham offered the boy in **faith**, not *fear*, not *confusion*, and not in *hesitancy.* He saw the one thing that could allow him to boldly ascend that mountain with a knife and some wood with which to sacrifice his son. The confusion was gone. He and the boy were going up that mountain, and he and the boy were coming back down that mountain. Resurrection made it all possible.

The test was not *"Do you love Me?"*

The test was not *"Will you obey Me?"*

The test was ***"Do you believe in resurrection?"*** It was a test that the Lord made sure Abraham would pass. It was kind of like an open book test. God would reveal the answer. Again, it would be the Lord's ability that would empower Abraham for obedience.

God had very specific reasons for this test. It was important to the Lord that Abraham knew about resurrection.

In this place called resurrection, Abraham would find the place of ultimate and absolute provision. In fact, he called the place *"The-Lord-Will-Provide."* It was here that he received the blessing of multiplication. Instead of being the father of one son, Abraham would be the father of many nations.

"Blessing I will bless you and multiplying I will multiply your descendants as the stars of the heaven and as the sand which is on the seashore... In your seed all the nations of the earth shall be blessed, because you have obeyed My voice." - Genesis 22:17-18

Remember, the power to obey came from the Lord, not from Abraham's strength. It was resurrection that enabled him to follow through, just like it was resurrection that enabled Jesus to endure the cross.

So this test, or revelation, would take Abraham to another level of blessing, the ultimate level. This is what God wanted, and it's what He wants for each of us.

But there was another reason the Lord went to these great lengths to show Abraham the resurrection. The Lord needed this for something He was looking at far down the road. God was paving the way for Jesus to come to earth.

Ever since God put us in the Garden of Eden, He has operated through man's dominion. God's will is manifested when a man agrees with it. It's the power of agreement that Jesus spoke of.

The Lord's purpose was always that He would resurrect fallen man. God had a man in Abraham who would agree with Him when the man saw resurrection. This would release the will of the Lord to be manifested.

"Surely the Lord God does nothing, unless He reveals His secret to His servants..." - Amos 3:7

"The secret things belong to the Lord our God, but those things which are revealed belong to us..." - Deuteronomy 29:29

The Resurrection would come to us, his name is Jesus.

*"Abraham rejoiced to see My day, **and he saw it** and was glad."* - John 8:56

Isn't this exactly what happened? Abraham saw the resurrection and got happy. It was bigger than his questions, his fears, and his confusion. It would cover any losses that he might incur during this test.

Resurrection makes any problem, even death itself look small. Resurrection is the power that overcomes this world. Resurrection is in us!

Resurrection is not just a date on a calendar way off into the future. Resurrection is for now.

Resurrection!

CHAPTER 6

Resurrection in Earth Life

"I am the resurrection…" -John 11:25

When Jesus announced that He was the resurrection, He was correcting an error in Martha's thinking. Jesus told her that her brother, Lazarus, would live again. She said she knew that. She knew he would live again someday in the resurrection at the last day.

But Jesus let her know that the resurrection was not a calendar date, it was Him. He was the resurrection. He was present, and resurrection could be now.

If Christ abides in us, then resurrection is in us. The same Spirit that raised Him from the dead is now in us. It's not just something that's waiting at the finish line in the sweet bye and bye.

We do know that the dead rise, and that's great to know. It's great to know that to be absent from the body is to be present with the Lord. It takes the sting out of losing a loved one when we know these things.

But resurrection is for those of us still left on earth too! The Lord is the resurrection, and He lives in us that we would live a resurrected life on earth.

*"...present yourselves to God **as being alive from the dead...**"* -Romans 6:13

The Bible tells us of an instance when Jesus came into a house to pray for a sick young lady. When He got to the house He encountered the wailing noise of grief and mourning. The sound of hopelessness bounced off of the walls. The girl was dead, and the din declared it with authority.

Mr. Resurrection stood in the house and declared that the girl was not dead, only sleeping.

Was she dead or sleeping? Some say that the mourners only thought she was dead, that she was really barely breathing, or in a coma. Others say she was obviously dead and don't know why Jesus said she was sleeping.

I happen to think she was dead. I don't think the event would be recorded if she wasn't dead. The attitude Jesus had toward it gives us a great object lesson. If we are dead it's over, and only an extraordinary miracle can make us alive; but if we are asleep we only need to wake up.

"And they ridiculed him, but when He had put them all outside...
Then He took the child by the hand, and said to her... 'Little girl, I say to you, arise.'
Immediately the girl arose and walked..." -Mark 5:40-42

The wisdom of this world mocks and discredits the power of resurrection. This mocking makes us victims of circumstance and victims of our weakness. This is the kind of noise that would keep Christ from accomplishing fullness in our lives. I can imagine the mocking that went on in this situation:

"Sleeping!? Yeah, right. That's the soundest sleep I've ever seen." (hahaha)
"Hey you guys, let's be quiet so we won't wake the girl." (hahaha)
"Maybe she's only dreaming of being dead." (hahaha)

But the Lord did what He does. He did what He does in our "house." He drove out the noise, and when the noise was gone the voice of the Lord was all that was heard. The voice said what it always says, "arise." When the voice was heard, the girl arose. All she needed was to hear the voice of Mr. Resurrection.

If you need a resurrection in your life, if you need a comeback, if you need a new start, the answer is in this story. Just look at these facts:

1. Mr. Resurrection was in the house, but the girl was still dead. (You are the house and He is in you, but there may be too much noise of hopelessness and limitation going on inside.)

2. Mr. Resurrection drove out the noise. (This symbolizes the Christian growth that comes from mind renewal. The sound of Life is driving out the sound of defeat and victimization.)

3. When the voice of Mr. Resurrection became the dominant voice in the house, the girl arose. (We have that voice in us. Listen for it, because it will wake you up and get you going.)

This is what happened to me. I did not pull myself up by my bootstraps. I did not "will" myself to get up and go forward. I heard the voice of the One who lives in me. The Spirit says, "Arise!"

In only a matter of days I rose up. I put the past, the pain, and the loss behind me. Without missing a service I was preaching destiny with a stronger faith and conviction. Some people were amazed. Others were suspicious of my grasp on reality. I think it's a shame that quick recovery is seen as amazing *or* suspicious, especially in the body of Christ. We are not like the world. We are different. We are supernatural. We have a great advantage, even in the worst of situations, it's Christ in us. He's the glory and the lifter of our heads.

We are aware of this overcoming life when the voice of Christ can be heard in our hearts. That is when the noise of victimization and helplessness has been expelled from our minds.

Greater is He that's in me, than he that is in the world! I heard the voice of the Greater One telling me to get up. That was the trumpet of my resurrection! There was no way I could lay down, give up, or back off of my abundant life. My voice and my life would be strong. I would move forward.

But what would my life look like?

I didn't have a clue…

Resurrection!

CHAPTER 7

Don't Dismiss the Now By Missing Your Past

If God were to say to me, *"You've been through a lot and I would like to make it up to you. What can I do for you that would make things alright?"* I honestly could not think of a thing that would make it okay. I could not imagine any blessing that would compensate for what I had lost.

I knew I had a life ahead, but could it ever be as good as my past? I had the best wife, the best marriage, the best life. Why couldn't I have just kept that? It felt like I had unwillingly traded the best for, what? I didn't have a clue.

But I did have a word from the Lord, and this word was more than enough to excite me. He took me to the book of Haggai.

Living in a Place Called "Nothing"

The background for the book of Haggai is the rebuilding of the temple. About fifty years after the first temple was destroyed by the Babylonians, work on the second temple had begun. It was a resurrection of sorts. The foundation was laid with great celebration by the young, but it was a disappointment to others.

The older people had seen the first temple, and the foundation of the new temple was not as large. Not only that, but it would not have the Ark of the Covenant with its contents. They were taken or destroyed with the first temple. There would be no stone tablets of the law, no Aaron's rod, no golden pot of manna. Too many things were missing. This temple would not be nearly as glorious as the first, and they let the others know that.

This disappointment, along with the efforts of outsiders who opposed the building, helped to cause discouragement and apathy in rebuilding the temple. So the foundation sat empty and idle for the next fifteen years.

But then God used the prophets Zechariah and Haggai to inspire the people to start again. Through Haggai, the Lord said:

*"Who is left among you who saw this temple in its former glory? And how do you see it now? In comparison with it, is this not in your eyes as **nothing**?"* -Haggai 2:3

In my own life, I had the best. I was living in my glory years, but they came to an abrupt end. I could not imagine anything in my future that could be as good as what I had. In fact, I didn't want anything else. I wanted what I had lost.

I went from everything to nothing. It seemed that my whole life was gone. Everything to which I was accustomed was no longer there. I found myself in the land of nothing. Compared to what I had, this looked like nothing.

If you are reading this and you have, or are, experiencing similar feelings, I have good news for you. If it looks like your best days are in your past, I have good news for you.

The truth is, God doesn't have to make up for what was lost. God doesn't have to match what we had before. He has better plans. He can do more than we can ask or imagine!

God didn't have to give me something as good as what I had lost. He could do more than I could ask or imagine!

God did not have to give the Jews a temple as great as the former. He could do more than they could ask or imagine!

"The glory in this latter temple shall be greater than the former..." -Haggai 2:9

The house did not have to be the same as the one in their past. The **glory** would be greater!

Maybe your past situation looks better than your present situation. It's okay, for even in a different situation the **glory** can be greater.

Immediately after Teresa left, my past definitely looked better than my present as far as the circumstances were concerned. In fact my circumstances looked like a lot of nothing; but God didn't have to replicate or equal my former situation. Whatever my situation would be in the days ahead, the glory would be greater!

This was the word that sealed it for me. I didn't have to demand a great situation from God. Whatever He had for me, the glory would be greater than anything I had known!

I still could not imagine any blessing or situation that would be as good as what I had lost, but I knew God, and He had something that was better than I could ask or imagine. I honestly didn't care anymore. I had God, and whether I would be single for life or remarried, rich or poor, it was of no concern to me. I had God, and the glory in my life would be greater than my "glory days."

Resurrection!

CHAPTER 8

The God I Knew
And the Future I Didn't

Teresa and I always had plans to return to Florida eventually. We loved it there. I spent many years growing up there. We had pastored a church and raised our family there. My ministry took me there many times a year.

Among my first decisions in this new and different time in my life, was the decision to get back to Florida quickly so I could be near my children and grandchildren. I was making trips to central Florida anticipating my new season. I began prepping to sell my house

During this time period something happened that I could not have imagined. Something happened that I didn't ask for, and couldn't have asked for, because I didn't know it existed. It was something, or rather *someone* that was so good and so right for me.

I met Judi. She was passionate about Jesus, had served in ministry for years on the mission field, and sounded much like myself when she spoke of the Lord. We seemed to have everything in common. We liked all the same things, and we seemed like old friends from our very first conversation.

We began talking every chance we got. We spoke from our computers, via text and phone calls.

When I was in Florida we would go out on special dates that always seemed magical. I took her to church to hear me speak, and she loved it. Soon, I was picking her up in the morning and taking her to work, meeting her for lunch, and picking her up at work again – like every day! We didn't want to be apart.

It didn't seem possible that I could be so happy this soon. I had fallen in love, and life was bright and good. Who gets two chances at this? Some don't get one shot at real love. And who gets a second chance so quickly?

It didn't seem fair. This was too good, and I spoke much with the Lord about it. He just continued to smile upon me and encourage me to be the shining example of life that He wanted me to be. In other words, just accept the blessing and favor of the Lord.

When You're Blessed, You're Blessed

My friends please listen to me. Your situation does not define who you are. A bad circumstance does not mean that you are cursed. You are defined by the Lord in you. You can be thrown into a pit, but if you're blessed, you will come out of the pit. When you're blessed, you're blessed!

I had experienced something horrible, but it didn't change the fact that I had blessing and favor. God was my blessing. I didn't turn from the One who was my blessing just because of a terrible situation. In fact, I turned *to* Him. This is how we not only survive, but thrive in any situation!

In my new season, I was totally prepared to accept whatever the Lord had for me. Whether I would remain single for the rest of my life, or He had someone for me to marry, it didn't matter. I would be happy.

I had loved being married to Teresa. She was a wonderful wife to me, and being her husband was a joy. I had no bad feelings or baggage from our marriage. On the contrary, I thoroughly loved our life together. Teresa made marriage so wonderful that I had no qualms about doing it again.

So it wasn't long before I asked Judi to marry me. She accepted and we had a beautiful wedding. It was an amazing day. My daughters stood with her and I was so happy. I was not nervous at all. Judi was what I really liked, and I knew who I wanted to be with for the rest of my life. She was the one who would walk with me the rest of the way home.

My marriage to Judi has been the most heavenly experience. God has proved Himself faithful by making the latter joy exceedingly greater than the former pain.

Another manifestation of God's resurrection power is the way He allowed me to pay off all debts so that I could enjoy a fresh start and a new season.

I was left with an overwhelming amount of medical debt from the years of fighting cancer. Not only that, but there was a lot of credit card debt from trying to live with such expenses. I had tried everything I knew to pay the debt, including seeking help from the avenues recommended by friends, but nothing was happening and I was making no real progress.

Then, only months after Judi and I were married, the Lord spoke to me and said, *"I will not be in debt."*

I quickly replied, *"You're not. I am."*

Then God said, *"No. We are one, and I won't be in debt. We are walking out of this."*

When I heard that, I knew it was done! I was out of town, so I called Judi and we celebrated on the phone.

In the next two weeks deals came together. We sold one of our houses for a BIG profit. (It was a house that a realtor told me I would have to take a loss on.) I negotiated my debts and was able to pay them all off!

WOOHOO!

No matter what you've gone through, or what you are going through, God has a resurrection for you!

Resurrection!

CHAPTER 9

Resurrection Covers Your Losses

As long as you have breath in your body, God has good things ahead for you. Lift up your eyes and see that it's not over. Your best is not behind you. It's in front of you. Maybe you've walked in a dark place, but that means that the shadow is on your back and the sun is on your face!

Have you ever noticed God's pattern of things getting better and not worse? Let me show you something.

We've already looked at God's promise to make the glory of the latter greater than the glory of the former. That was enough to get me excited about my future, but here are some more biblical examples of the same divine pattern.

"...the evening and the morning were the first day." -Genesis 1:5

In God's creation, a day doesn't start in the morning and end at night. Instead, it begins with darkness and ends in light. It gets brighter, not darker! Not only that, but we also see in this same passage of creation that the earth begins without form, and God makes something beautiful. He is doing that in your life too!

"...this Child is destined for the fall and rising of many in Israel..." -Luke 2:34

Many people quote this and say "the **rise** and **fall**", putting the rise *before* the fall. Such a phrase is used in many quotes and books, but the bible puts the *fall* first and the *rising* second. Even in the story of mankind, we see an immediate fall, then an eventual rising. The latter is greater than the former!

"...the path of the just is like the shining sun that shines brighter unto the perfect day." -Proverbs 4:18

It burns brighter, not dimmer!

"...the spiritual is not first, but the natural, and afterward the spiritual." - I Corinthians 15:46

This speaks of God's pattern from the first Adam to the last Adam (Jesus). The latter is greater. It's always like that!

Of course, it's also the pattern of our own lives. We are born natural. We are born again spiritual. Our latter is better than our beginning.

Also, look at verse 49:

"And as we have borne the image of the man of dust, we shall also bear the image of the heavenly Man."
- I Corinthians 15:49

There it is. It's the same pattern. God's way is simply to increase, multiply, spread out, and get better and better. If you have received Christ, that pattern is set into your life!

"...Every man at the beginning sets out the good wine, and when the guests have well drunk, then the inferior. You have kept the good wine until now!"
- John 2:10

This was the statement made about Jesus when He turned water into wine. Of **course** He saved the best for last! That's just what He does. It's his pattern of doing things, and it's the pattern determined for your life.

Then of course, there is the resurrection of Jesus. He was amazing in His earthly walk, loving, forgiving, healing, teaching, and meeting needs. Those who loved Him were devastated by His death. It looked like things would never be as good as when Jesus was alive. However, His resurrection made things better than his disciples could have imagined, far better!

The power of His resurrection in you is what covers all of your losses. It means that God has something better than you can imagine. His life in you is more powerful than any loss, any pain. It's real, and it is making you a sign and a wonder. Let the people around you watch and see how wonderful God can be.

I've written this book to help with your heavenly vision. Where there is no vision, we perish; but *with* vision, we thrive!

I am a witness that God is faithful and true, and He can be trusted. I am happier than I've ever been, and I've never loved God more. I have a message of glorious hope that I want to shout from the housetops.

If you are going through a difficult time, or you have gone through one, and the past has seemed better than your future; get ready to be surprised. This book is not in your hand by accident!

"...the sufferings of this present time are not worthy to be compared with the glory which shall be revealed... " - Romans 8:18

Arise and shine for your light has come, and the glory of the Lord is on you. Let those around you watch and see how wonderful God is.

Your latter is greater than your former!

The shadow is on your back, and the sun is on your face!

Wonderful things are in your path, and God has saved the best wine for last!

Forward, guys!

Resurrection!

About the Author

MINISTRY

Rick is a spirit-filled minister, event speaker, and motivator. He is a mentor and advisor to many Christian leaders. Countless lives have been transformed as he has preached and taught thousands of speaking engagements.

Using personal examples of faith adventures, self-effacing humor, and a clear lifestyle example, Rick leads and encourages people to experience the Kingdom of Heaven in this life. His message is that God has given us all we need in Jesus Christ, and if we believe, we can enjoy every bit of it.

Because Rick has an ability to relate to all types of people, he is invited to many different kinds of groups, churches and organizations.

LIFESTYLE

Rick is a youthful, vibrant 50-something, who hasn't had the flu or a headache since 1982.

The Lord has blessed him with prosperity and success as a minister, family man, and businessman.

Rick and his wife, Judi, make their home in beautiful central Florida.

HISTORY, BACKGROUND & EXPERIENCE

- Saved from a life of drugs, alcohol abuse and crime in 1979 at the age of 21.
- Attended Rhema Bible Training Center in '83-'84.
- Associate Pastor '84-'88.
- Pastor '89-'98.
- Itinerant Minister '98-present.

If you liked *"RESURRECTION! Trusting the God I Knew With a Future I Didn't,"* you will love these other books by Rick Manis:

"FULLNESS! *Living Beyond Revivals & Outpourings*"

This book may be the push that you need to help you complete the transition from the highs and lows of the past move and into the consistent, glory filled life you have been promised!

"The Now Zone"

Waiting on God? Or is God waiting on you? This book will help you lose the wait, so you can bring your tomorrow into today.

"Glory in the Glass"

Meet your heavenly self! When you see who you really are, you will find it is better than all of your hopes and dreams.

Order online at Rickmanis.com
Or call toll free: 877-407-9331

Also available at Amazon.com, BarnesandNoble.com, and other major booksellers

You may also be interested in:

"Heaven on Earth University"

This *Life Mastery Course* is an audio curriculum you can study at home at your own pace.

Learn to master the human experience with this interactive study system that deals with every area of life.

The curriculum includes:

- 18 Lessons
- 8 CD's
- Workbook
- Graduation Certificate

All for $50!

Order online at Rickmanis.com

Or call toll free: 877-407-9331

Made in the USA
San Bernardino, CA
09 June 2015